Circle five things that are **wrong** with this picture

Draw a line from each picture to where it **belongs**.

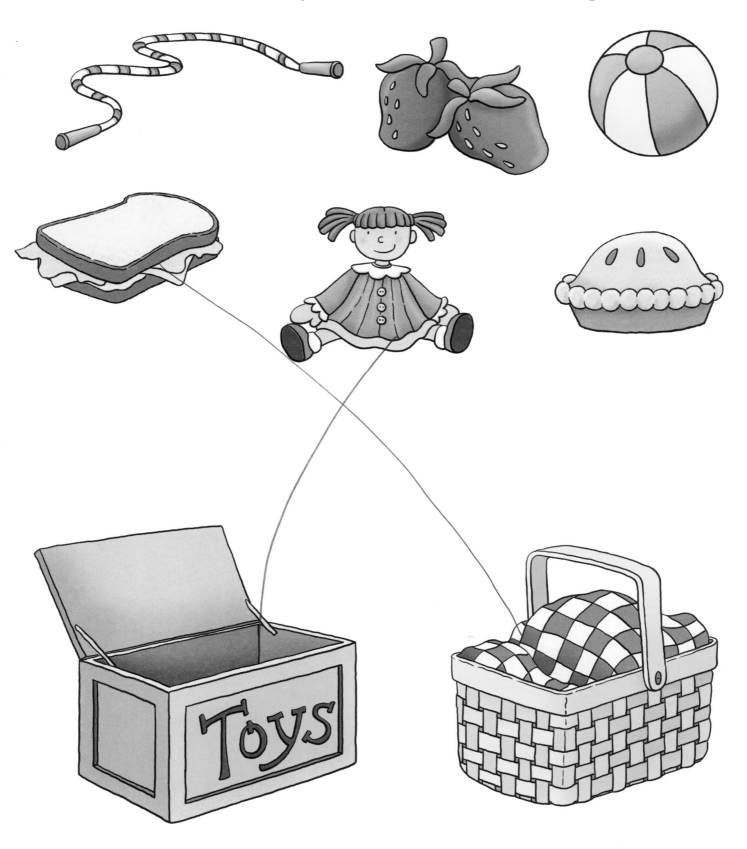

Draw a line from each picture to where it belongs.

Circle the picture that **does not** belong.

Circle the picture that does not belong.

Write **1** by what happened **first**.
Write **2** by what happened **next**.
Write **3** by what happened **last**.

Write **1** by what happened **first**.
Write **2** by what happened **next**.
Write **3** by what happened **last**.

Write **1** by what happened **first**.
Write **2** by what happened **next**.
Write **3** by what happened **last**.

Circle 2 that are the same.

Circle 2 that are the same in each group.

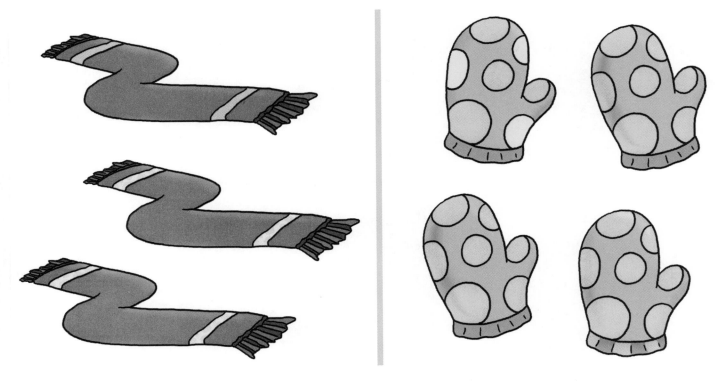

Circle the letters that are the **same** as the first two.

AC	FG	AC
BB	BB	OO
DE	EE	DE
KF	KR	KF

Circle the picture in each row that is **different**.

  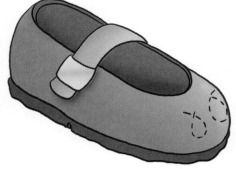

What **belongs** in each box?
Draw the shapes in the correct color.

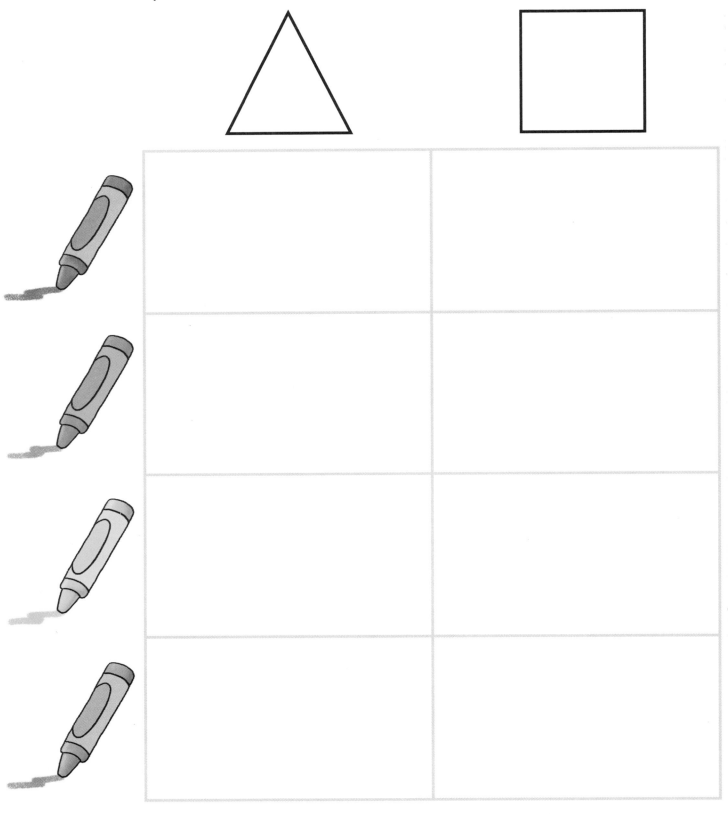

What belongs in each box?
Draw the shapes in the correct color.

Draw a line from each hat to its box.

Draw a line from each cookie cutter to
its cookie.

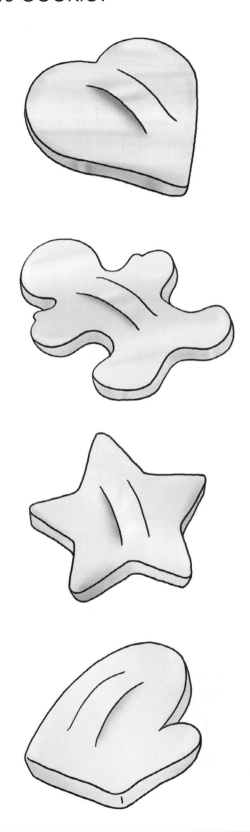

Draw a line from the dollhouse to the
box that has its furniture.

Circle two pictures that **go together** in each row.

Draw the shape that comes **next**.

 _____

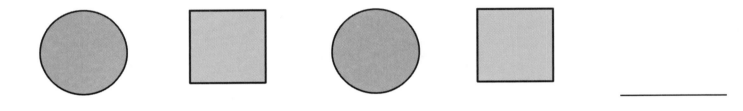 _____

 _____

Draw what comes next.

_____

_____

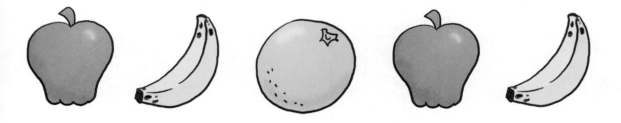

_____

Circle the picture that completes the sentence.

 is to  as  is to _____ .

 is to  as  is to _____ .

Circle the picture that completes the sentence.

 is to 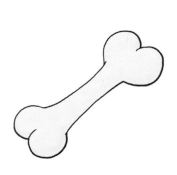 as  is to _____ .

 is to  as  is to _____ .

Which pet did Mia choose?
Circle the correct picture.

1. It cannot fly.

2. It is not gray.

3. It has a long tail.

Which house is Peter's?
Circle the correct picture.

1. It has a green door.

2. It is not pink.

3. It has two windows.

Which snowman did Jamal make?
Circle the correct picture.

1. It has a blue hat.

2. It does not have a coat.

3. It has a blue tie.

Which frog did John keep?
Circle the correct picture.

1. It has spots.

2. It does not have purple on it.

3. It has yellow on it.

Read the clues.
Draw a line from the name to the correct clown.

1. Mac is between Ned and Jake.

2. Jake has a flower in his hat.

Ned   Jake   Mac

Read the clues.
Draw a line from the name to the correct dog.

1. Hero is on the bottom.

2. Rags is in the middle.

3. Paco is under Duke.

4. Where is Fido?

Rags

Duke

Paco

Hero

Fido

Put an X by the picture that shows why this happened.

28

Put an **X** by the picture that shows why this happened.

Read the directions.
Match them to the correct row.

A

Cross out what we can eat.

C

B

Circle what is alive.

_____

C

Circle what we can eat and underline what we can wear.

_____

D

Cross out the cat and underline the shoes.

_____

30

Read the directions.
Match them to the correct row.

A

Cross out what is **not** alive.

_____

B

Circle the animals and put an X on the toys.

_____

C

Circle what lays eggs and underline the ball.

_____

D

Circle the cow and underline the doll.

_____

Circle the picture that shows how you would **feel**.

Draw what is **missing** in the picture.

Circle what you can do in summer.

Circle what you can do in winter.

Look at the pictures until you can **remember** them.
Turn to page 38.

Circle five things that are **wrong** with this picture.

Circle **only** the pictures you **remember** from page 36.
No peeking!

Circle what is **alive**.

Circle the items you can **smell**.

Circle what you can taste.

Circle the items you can **touch**.

Circle what you can **hear**.

How many people are going left?_____

How many cars are going **right**? _____

Circle the things that **could not** happen.

Circle what comes **next**.

A B A B A B

A
B

AB CD AB

AB
CD

Look at clown A.
Circle 7 things that are **different** on clown B?

clown A

clown B

Look at the scene below.
Circle the five hidden images.

Draw a line to the picture that shows **why** this happened.

50

Circle the picture that shows what will happen **next**.

How many of each?
Guess. Then count.

My Guess

How Many?

Count.
Color the graph to show **how many** of each kind.

	1	2	3	4	5

| 1 | 2 | 3 | 4 | 5 |

Look at the pictures in each row.
One thing will be the **same** in all rows.
Circle the sentence that tells what is the
same in each row.

1. The first car has a flat tire.

2. The last car has a bent bumper.

3. The middle car is the same color.

Look at the pictures in each row.
One thing will be the **same** in all rows.
Circle the sentence that tells what is the
same in each row.

1. All apples are red.

2. All rows have a pineapple.

3. The last fruit in each row is a banana.

Color by letters to show a picture and word.

This is a picture of a _____ .

A = **purple**   B = **red**   C = orange   D = green   E = **blue**

Color by letters to show a picture and word.

This is a picture of a _____ .

A = yellow   B = brown   C = **black**   D = red   E = blue

Underline the one thing you **do not need**.

1. To catch a fish, you need:

   a fishing pole

   a boat

   worms

2. To make a bird house, you need:

   bird seed

   nails

   wood

3. To cook an egg, you need:

   a stove

   a pan

   a sink

4. To see a movie, you need:

   money

   a hat

   a ticket

Use the grid on the map to find the treasure.

Find the clock.
Start at 0. Go across to E and up to 1.

Circle the treasure you find at the letters and numbers below.

1. C, 4

2. E, 1

3. B, 0

4. C, 2

Answers

Page 1

Page 2

Page 3

Page 4

Page 5

Page 6

Page 7

Page 8

Page 9

Page 10
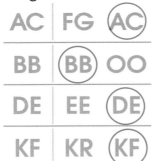

Page 11
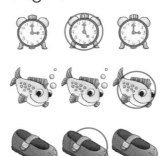

Page 12
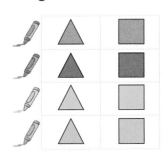

Page 13
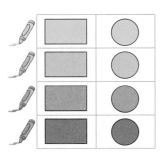

Page 14

Page 15

Page 16

Page 17

Page 18

Drawing should be;

Row 1: diamond

Row 2: circle

Row 3: star

Page 19

Drawing should be;

Row 1: lily pad

Row 2: carrot

Row 3: orange

Page 20

Page 21

Page 22

Page 23

Page 24

Page 25

Page 26

Ned   Jake   Mac

Page 27

Rags

Duke

Paco

Hero

Fido

Page 28

Page 29

Page 30

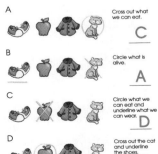

A — Cross out what we can eat. **C**

B — Circle what is alive. **A**

C — Circle what we can eat and underline what we can wear. **D**

D — Cross out the cat and underline the shoes. **B**

Page 31

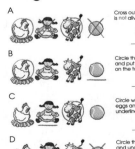

A — Cross out what is not alive. **D**

B — Circle the animals and put an X on the toys. **A**

C — Circle what lays eggs and underline the ball. **B**

D — Circle the cow and underline the doll. **C**

Page 32

Page 33

Child should have drawn in:

Umbrella handle

Back tire on car

Door on house

Dog house roof

Page 34

Page 35

Page 37

Page 38

Child should have circled:

boy playing soccer

girl doing handstand

girl writing on paper

boy eating apple

Page 39

Page 40

Page 41

Page 42

Page 43

Page 44

There are **5** people walking left.

Page 45

There are **3** cars going right.

Page 46

Page 47

A B A B A B (A) B

AB CD AB AB (CD)

Page 48

Child should have circled:

1. flower in hat
2. purple hair
3. eye direction
4. suspenders
5. three buttons
6. pink socks
7. triangles on stand

Page 49

Page 50

Page 51

Page 52

My Guess	may vary			
How Many?	4	2	3	5

Page 53

1 2 3 4 5

Page 54

1. The first car has a flat tire.

2. The last car has a bent bumper.

3. The middle car is the same color.

Page 55

1. All apples are red.

2. All rows have a pineapple.

3. The last fruit in each row is a banana.

Page 56

Page 57

Page 58

1. a boat

2. bird seed

3. a sink

4. a hat

Page 59

1. C, 4

2. E, 1

3. B, 0

4. C, 2

Write your name on the certificate.

Great Job!

YIPPEE!

first name:

last name:

has completed **Thinking Skills** from School Zone Publishing.

RAH

HOORAY